Peer Mediation

THE COMPLETE GUIDE TO RESOLVING
CONFLICT IN OUR SCHOOLS

Peer Mediation

THE COMPLETE GUIDE TO RESOLVING CONFLICT IN OUR SCHOOLS

HETTY VAN GURP

PORTAGE & MAIN PRESS

02 03 04 05 06 5 4 3 2 1

**National Library of Canada
Cataloguing in Publication Data**

Van Gurp, Hetty.

      Peer mediation
      ISBN 1-55379-001-4

1. Peer counseling of students. 2. Mediation. 3. Conflict management. I. Title.
LB 1027.5.V32 2002   371.4'047   C2002-910477-7

"The Puzzling Case" from *Peace in the Classroom*, by Hetty Adams,
1994, Peguis Publishers Ltd., Winnipeg is reprinted with permission.

Portage & Main Press acknowledges the financial support of the Government
of Canada through the Book Publishing Industry Development Program
for our publishing activities.

Book and cover design: Gallant Design Ltd.
Author photo: Michelle McMinn

Printed and bound in Canada by Kromar Printing Ltd.

**PORTAGE &
MAIN PRESS**
(formerly Peguis Publishers)

100 – 318 McDermot Avenue
Winnipeg, Manitoba, Canada R3A 0A2
E-mail: books@peguis.com
Tel: 204-987-3500
Toll free: 800-667-9673
Fax: 866-734-8477

*This book is dedicated to
the memory of Emmet Fralick.*

ContentsContents

PrefacePreface

In recent years, the media have presented evidence of an alarming increase in both the number and nature of violent offences committed by young people. A number of theories attempt to explain this trend: from changing family structure and the glorification of violence on television and in movies, to unemployment and poverty. The problem of increased violence among young people is one that concerns us all. Both formal and informal surveys indicate that, as a result of these news stories, many students feel intimidated or unsafe in school; others, unfortunately, learn that violence is a newsworthy option.

There is ongoing debate about solutions. Some people believe that we should "get tough" and impose more severe punishments. The "zero tolerance" approach has gained acceptance in many schools. Inherent in this approach is often a "no questions asked" policy and an immediate suspension as a response to predetermined offences.

If we believe that we will achieve peace simply by mandating it, imposing it, or temporarily banishing perpetrators, then we may also wish to hang a poster of Einstein on our bedroom wall in the hopes of waking up brilliant! As history sadly demonstrates, this approach simply does not work. Writing stricter policies and rules, imposing suspensions, detentions and expulsions only partially address the issue of violating school rules. They do not address the students' inability to resolve conflict effectively and often result in repeat offences. Although well-meaning teachers and administrators spend hours dealing with various interpersonal conflicts, due to the limited amount of time available to each 'problem,' many of the conflicts are often left unresolved.

One long-term solution is to create an environment in which aggressive behaviours of any kind are considered socially unacceptable, not only by authority figures but by students, teachers and parents. Since schools are often the only stable influence in the lives of many young people today, educators are beginning to realize that, for everyone's benefit, it is incumbent upon them to equip students with the attitudes, knowledge and skills they need to become responsible, fully participating citizens. Against the backdrop of an increasingly violent society, many schools have sought out innovative programs to teach young people effective strategies to live in harmony with one another.

Peer mediation is one of these programs. Students from the age of nine can learn the principles and practices of mediation to help their peers resolve conflict in a creative and peaceful manner with little need for adult intervention. A school-based peer mediation program that promotes "win-win" problem solving provides an effective alternative to traditional responses to conflict. When I was a school principal, my job was made a lot easier due to having a group of capable, insightful and willing mediators to deal with the conflicts that occurred daily in our school.

A peer mediation program is most effective when it is part of a school-wide, proactive approach to dealing with conflict. My personal experience with peer mediation goes back to 1991 when I first organized training camps in Nova Scotia. Several schools would collaborate and plan a training session to run over a weekend in a local outdoor camp setting. Those are very memorable days. Some of the students who were trained as school mediators during that time have now gone on to study in related fields at university. From reports I have received from them and from their parents, the experience made a positive and lasting impact on them and on their families. One father proudly told me that three of his children had been chosen to become mediators and one was now studying mediation at university.

If you have purchased this book, it is likely that you would like to "do something" to alleviate student conflict and work towards a more peaceful school environment. I hope the information given here will answer your needs and lead to your desired goals.

A SUCCESS STORY

Cole Harbour High is a Canadian school that received unexpected national notoriety. In 2000 the school closed its doors for a week after a violent incident that left the students and staff disheartened and struggling to find a way to address the underlying cause of the violence.

In an attempt to deal with the problems in a proactive manner, one of the strategies adopted at Cole Harbour was to initiate a peer mediation program. Linda Thieu was one of the founding members of Cole Harbour's peer mediation program and served as a mediator until her graduation.

Linda was also valedictorian for her graduating class at Cole Harbour High in 2001. As I had had the privilege of training Linda and her peers in mediation, I felt a sense of pride when I read about her in the local newspaper. In her valedictory she said, *"Our principal said…if we were to have one more big fight, our school would be shut down. Our peer mediation program, which brings students together to talk about their problems, is what has kept the school together."*[1]

Another Cole Harbour student wrote about the confidentiality of the mediation process based on her experience as a disputant. *"The aspect that surprised me the most was the respect and confidentiality of the student mediators. Sure, that's their job but how tempting is it to be involved firsthand in some of the school's juiciest gossip? Our team of mediators take their vows of confidentiality and respect as seriously as any paid professional."*[2]

---

1. "She goes about making things better," Sarah McGinnis. *The Chronicle Herald*, Halifax, Nova Scotia. July 4, 2001.

2. "Hippie Crap or a Real Solution?" Kim McKay. *Peace of Mind*, February 1999 (the newsletter of the League of Peaceful Schools).

IntroductionIntroduction

Peer mediation is a voluntary process for resolving conflict. Students who have been trained in mediation assist those students in dispute to reach a mutually agreeable solution to their conflict. The role of the peer mediators is to help the disputants find a "win-win" solution. They do not judge or counsel but simply listen carefully while each disputant tells his/her side of the story. Then the peer mediators encourage the disputants to come up with ideas to resolve the conflict.

Certain skills required in mediation can be taught. Students can learn to be good listeners, to summarize what they hear and to ask open questions. In addition to these learned skills, students chosen to be peer mediators need to have certain personal qualities and characteristics. Students who show concern for others, are fair, calm and have a natural tendency to be good listeners usually make successful peer mediators.

Mediation is:

A voluntary process

A process to help solve conflicts between two or more people

A process by which the disputants decide on their own solutions to the conflict

A process in which the disputants feel the solutions are fair

A process in which everyone is shown respect

A process which works on the concept of fairness rather than power

A process that respects the confidentiality of the people involved

There are many advantages to having peer mediation operating in your school. The benefits accrue directly to students and all school staff and secondarily to parents and the entire education program. The following ten point list is adapted from one originally published by the National Association for Mediation in Education (NAME), based at 425 Amity Street, Amherst, MA 01002, and is used here with permission.

Ten Good Reasons to Establish a Mediation Program

1. Conflict is natural. It is better approached with solutions than avoidance.

2. In schools, more appropriate and effective responses to conflict than detention, suspension, expulsion and court intervention are needed.

3. The use of mediation to resolve school-based disputes can result in improved communication between and among students, teachers, administrators and parents and can, in general, improve the school climate as well as provide a forum for addressing common concerns.

4. The use of mediation as a conflict resolution method can result in a reduction of violence, vandalism, chronic school absence and suspension.

5. Mediation training helps both elementary students and teachers deepen their understanding about themselves and others and provides them with lifelong conflict resolution skills.

6. Mediation training increases students' interests in conflict resolution, justice, and the legal system.

7. Shifting the responsibility for solving appropriate school conflict from adults to young adults and children frees both teachers and administrators to concentrate more on teaching than on discipline.

8. Recognizing that young people are competent to participate in the resolution of their own disputes encourages student growth and gives students skills such as listening, critical thinking and problem solving that are basic to all learning.

9. Mediation training, with its emphasis on listening to others' points of view and the peaceful resolution of differences, assists in preparing students to live in a diverse world.

10. Mediation provides a system of problem solving that is uniquely suited to the personal nature of young people's problems and is frequently used by students for problems they would not take to an adult.

The peer mediation activities described in this book have been well tested and modified since the early 1990s. The program was written for use in elementary schools; however, the activities are suitable for both elementary and secondary. For training secondary students, you may wish to make modifications or additions to the training activities. For example, the role-plays might be rewritten to better reflect typical high school conflicts.

When designing a training agenda you will need to consider several factors: your level of comfort and your prior experience with peer mediation, the level of experience of the students selected, how well the students know one another, your personal style and the time frame of the training session.

The training activities are divided into four sections:

Getting Acquainted,

The Nature of Conflict,

Communication Skills, and

The Mediation Process.

Within each section there are several activities. Do not feel that you need to include all of the activities in your training session. A variety is included in each section so that you can choose those most relevant to your group of students.

Chapter 1

Starting a Peer Mediation Program

This chapter considers the questions you must answer when contemplating the implementation of a peer mediation program. **In my experience, it is not possible for a handful of enthusiastic teachers to initiate such a program without an understanding of the program by school administrators, and their full commitment to its success.**

The following questions will be considered:

1. How will we introduce the concept of peer mediation to staff members?

2. How will we create awareness between students and community members?

3. How will students be selected to be peer mediators?

4. How will the training be conducted?

5. When, where, and how will mediation sessions take place?

6. Which issues will be referred to mediation?

7. How will the program be maintained?

1. Introducing the concept of peer mediation to staff

The success of a peer mediation program depends, to a great extent, on the support of the school administrative team. Although it does not take too many enthusiastic teachers to initiate, implement, and supervise the program, without administrative understanding and support the eventual demise of the program is inevitable.

An introductory session for staff members (including all support staff) is vital. Many schools have successful mediation programs in place. Try to find one to assist with such a session. When training, I often begin an awareness session by reading the following true story. It happened one day during my first year as a vice-principal. Anyone who has ever worked in a school setting (in northern climates) can undoubtedly relate to this scenario.

PICTURE IT

You are the principal of a middle school with an enrollment of 350 students. It's a slushy, cold day in February and just before lunchtime one of your duty supervisors called to let you know that she will not be in. Normally you would take her place and go outside yourself, but today you have a meeting scheduled with an irate parent so you asked one of the teachers to do lunch duty. Although she agreed, she mumbled something as she was putting on her boots.

Your meeting with the parents is not going well and you are becoming anxious as you realize that you have only 40 minutes to get to the Board office where you are giving an afternoon presentation to your colleagues.

The afternoon bell rings and, as you make an effort to draw your meeting to a conclusion, you become aware of a growing level of noise coming from the hall directly outside of your office. You excuse yourself to look out into the hall where you see nine students in wet clothing. Some are sitting on the bench and the remainder are leaning against the painted Valentine's Day mural that has already started to run and is now forming red and pink puddles on the floor. At this point, the lunch-duty teacher comes in with two more students, one of whom is yelling at the other — something about a destroyed snow fort. Glancing at the clock you realize that you could just make it to the Board Office in time if you left this very minute.

The purpose in reading this story at a staff orientation session is to illustrate, in an amusing way, the advantages of having students trained in peer mediation. Peer mediators can deal with the typical kind of conflict that occurs in most schools. If this school had had a peer mediation program in place, the line-up outside the principal's office need not have occurred. With mediation available to students, problems can be resolved as they occur with little need for adult intervention. (We started a peer mediation program shortly after this happened.)

The staff orientation session might include a brief overview of the advantages of establishing a peer mediation program, (see page 6) then a role-play to demonstrate the process, followed by a question and answer period.

Once support from staff has been generated, only a few key staff members are needed to coordinate the program. Some of the responsibilities of the coordinator(s) include:

- introducing the program to students and parents
- overseeing the selection of students to be peer mediators
- planning and participating in the training
- developing a duty schedule for the peer mediators
- holding regular meetings with the mediators
- keeping the school community informed of progress/new developments

2. Creating awareness among students and parents

As mentioned previously, one key to the successful implementation of a peer mediation program is an understanding of the program by all members of the school community.

After the initial introductory session for staff, students and parents must be informed of the school's plan to introduce a mediation program. This awareness-raising phase should take two to three weeks.

There are many ways to create awareness among members of the school community. Some ideas include:

- obtain or prepare a brochure on Peer Mediation

- mount articles and posters on school bulletin boards explaining the mediation process and the advantages of a peer mediation program

- prepare a letter to parents or a supplement to the regular parent newsletter

- prepare short skits to be presented to all classes

- plan and implement an evening presentation for parents

- if possible, obtain commercially prepared videos that demonstrate the mediation process and show to students, parents, and administrators

- stage a school-wide assembly with a presentation by an experienced "team"

- prepare a description of the program for inclusion in the School Discipline Policy

- prepare and place a monthly update in the school newsletter

Remember to maintain ongoing communication with parents in order to ensure that new families are made aware of the school's approach to dealing with student conflict.

3. Selecting students to be peer mediators

Being a peer mediator is strictly voluntary. In elementary school, students are usually selected from the upper grade levels. Ideally, the students who are chosen should represent a cross section of the student population. There should be an equal number of girls and boys. Make available the following list of criteria or guidelines.

A peer mediator should be:

- a good listener

- respected

- fair

- a good problem solver

- concerned about others
- able to communicate clearly
- a responsible student

Determine, by school size and conditions, the number of mediation teams needed. In my experience, a good ratio is one mediator for every 25 students. Then, select students by one or more of the following options:

a. Invite students to nominate classmates.

b. Encourage students to apply to become a peer mediator. (See pages 68-69 for sample application form and sample parents' permission form.)

c. Train an existing group (i.e. student council, safety club).

In most schools there are students who have good leadership skills; there are also students who display leadership skills who, unfortunately, seem to use their skills in a negative fashion. Consider offering a special invitation to one or more of these students to become trained in mediation: an opportunity to use their leadership abilities in a positive way can make a dramatic difference in the lives of these students.

4. Training the mediators

When introducing a peer mediation program, the initial training session should be conducted by someone with both training and experience in school-based mediation. Many questions will arise during the training that can best be addressed by someone with "hands-on" experience.

Although only a small team of staff members is needed to conduct the program after the training, ideally as many staff members as possible should attend the training in order to give them a broader understanding of the principles and practices of mediation. In subsequent years, the school coordinator usually plans and conducts the training sessions.

The initial training takes approximately 14-16 hours (2 days).

There are many options for planning training sessions: a two-day retreat (see Sample Training Agenda, pages 70-71); a weekend (on site); several after school sessions; or one full day followed by a few lunchtime or after school sessions. You will ultimately structure the training based on your own needs and the resources available.

A final decision regarding the training schedule is often based on funds available. If your school has a budget or a sponsor for this program, my personal experience indicates that a two-day retreat is an ideal setting for mediation training. Costs include rental of facility, meals, T-shirts (optional).

All of Chapters Two and Three cover the training process.

5. Choosing issues to be referred to mediation

Each school must decide which issues will be handled by the mediators and which will be dealt with by staff. As a general rule, most schools do not expect students to mediate issues regarding serious physical violence, drugs, weapons or abuse.

The majority of disputes are easily resolved through mediation if intervention takes place in the early stages. When a teacher, administrator or the program coordinator makes the referral, the school can keep an informal track of the nature of the conflict that is occurring in terms of frequency, type, and disputants involved.

One point about which I feel very strongly is the need for adult intervention when making a decision about whether or not the issue should be referred to mediation. It is unfair to expect students to intervene in a schoolyard conflict and be expected to make a decision about how it should be handled. All mediations should be arranged by an adult.

In the high school mediation training model, the mediators explicitly state that, if the conflict involves alcohol, drugs or abuse, they will refer it to their program coordinator. In the elementary model, a responsible adult making the referral can divert such issues from the mediation process and ensure that school staff handles them.

Types of disputes that are appropriate for student mediation include:

- rumors/gossip

- damage to the property of others

- name-calling

- poor sportsmanship

- disputes around borrowing/returning

- minor scuffles, such as shoving, tripping, snowball throwing, etc.

6. The when, where, and how of mediation

When Usually, the program coordinator prepares a weekly or monthly duty schedule that is made known to all school staff members and students. Each day, one or two pairs of peer mediators (made up of boy/girl combinations) should be "on call" or "on duty." There is no need for these peer mediators to sit and wait for referrals. They should continue to engage in their regular activities and make themselves available as they are needed.

The school staff will need to decide whether mediation sessions take place exclusively at recess, lunch or after school or whether, at times, they can occur during class time. Naturally, there are both advantages and disadvantages to conducting mediation sessions during class time and this is ultimately a school-based decision. My personal belief is that a conflict is best resolved as soon as possible after it occurs; when two students are sitting in class seething about the argument they had at recess, chances are they will not be in a learning attitude anyway.

Where Ideally, the mediation program should have a designated room within the school. In the reality of overcrowded schools, however, this is not always possible. It is important that mediation sessions take place in close proximity to teacher supervision in case the mediators need assistance.

How Mediation sessions are usually conducted in private without the need for an adult to be in the room. This helps preserve the confidentiality of the sessions and also makes it easier for the disputants to speak openly and honestly.

7. Maintaining the program

After the training session, the program coordinator usually meets with the mediators on a regular basis to develop skills further and discuss problems that arise. It is vital to the success of a school-based mediation program that the mediators remain motivated and busy. After every mediation session, the mediators involved complete a report form. These reports provide a useful record of the types of conflict that occur, the students involved and whether or not the conflicts were resolved. A sample is provided (see page 72), but your school may want to create its own.

When the mediation process is unsuccessful because the disputants are not able or willing to resolve their dispute, it should be referred to the coordinator. At this stage, schools usually have an internal strategy in place to deal with the conflict.

As long as school staff members have a solid understanding of the mediation process and the school's policy regarding implementation and show their support by making referrals for mediation, no further time commitment on the part of staff is necessary.

If you find that the number of referrals for mediation begins to decline, as will happen, you may wish to consider other ideas for engaging the mediators in meaningful ways. For example, at one school the mediators develop and offer "lessons in living" presentations for classes in the school. These are lessons in effective communication, appreciating diversity, expressing emotions, and so on. The mediators provide the teachers with a brief description of the "lesson of the week" and post a sign-up sheet on the refrigerator in the staff room. There is usually a rush to sign up when the notice is posted! The mediators arrive at the designated time complete with props, hand-outs and anything else they may need to make the lesson interesting and inspiring for the students.

Chapter 2
Training the Mediators

First, review the general comments about training on page 13 in Chapter One.

In the following pages, you will find a number of training activities divided into the following sections:

Getting Acquainted

The Nature of Conflict

Communication Skills

The Mediation Process

For each training session, choose a number of activities from the pertinent section based on your individual preference. As well, you may have activities that you have used successfully and that seem appropriate. Be creative and have fun!

The Name Game

Objective:

To provide an opportunity for participants to introduce themselves

You Will Need:

- chart paper and markers, or
- chalkboard and chalk

Directions:

1. Explain to students that this activity will give them an opportunity to introduce themselves and share some personal background information with the group.

2. Begin by printing your name on the chart paper. Tell the students something about yourself related to your name, i.e. who you were named after, why your parents chose your name, your nickname, or anything else!

3. Following your example, invite students to take turns printing their names crossword puzzle style (connected to the letters already on the paper) and sharing a similar type of information.

Example:

```
H E N D R I K A
        L
        Y           D
        S A M A N T H A
        O           M
        N           I
                    E
                    N
```

> **Lesson:** Sometimes we do not
> know our classmates as well as we think.

Web Game

Objectives:

To enable students to become acquainted with one another

To create a friendly atmosphere

To enhance listening skills

You Will Need:

- a ball of yarn

Directions:

1. Ask students to stand in a circle.

2. Explain that each person will have an opportunity to throw the ball of yarn to someone he/she does not know (or know well). To demonstrate, throw the ball of yarn to someone, introduce yourself to that person and tell one thing you like to do. (Make sure you hold onto your end of the yarn!)

3. When everyone has introduced her/himself, use the following questions for discussion:

    "What have we formed?"

    "How is communication like a web?" (goes from one person to another, sometimes gets tangled)

    "What happens if I pull my end of the yarn?"(others feel the tension)

    "How are people affected when a participant is angry or upset?"

4. Reverse the process. The last person to receive the ball of yarn begins and as the ball is passed, tries to remember and say the receiving person's name and what he/she likes to do.

5. Discuss: *"How did you feel when you first joined the circle?"* *"How do you feel now?"*

> **Lesson:** As mediators you will be expected to make students feel comfortable. Using their names will make them feel respected.

Getting to Know You Bingo

Objective:

To help participants become acquainted with one another in an interactive manner

You Will Need:

- copies of "Getting to Know You Bingo" (see page 74)
- pencils

Directions:

1. Explain to students that the goal of this activity is to complete the Bingo sheet by circulating through the group, matching participants with the descriptions.

2. Make it clear that each student may sign her/his name only once.

3. Instruct the students to call "Bingo!" when their sheets are completed.

4. When most of the students have completed the activity, use the following questions to guide a discussion:

   "Have you learned anything about each other?"

   "Were you surprised by anything you learned?"

Lesson: When people have things in common,
it becomes easier to communicate.

Trading Places

Objective:

To provide an opportunity for students to meet a few members of the group

You Will Need:

■ nametags

■ pens or markers

Directions:

1. Ask each participant to write his/her name on a nametag.

2. Ask each participant to pair up with a person he/she does not know and spend approximately two minutes telling each other about themselves (as much as each person can share in one minute).

3. When time is up, the people in each pair exchange nametags. The participants now choose a different partner. This time they introduce themselves as the person whose nametag they are wearing, using all the information that was told to them by their previous partner.

4. Once again, after two minutes, the individuals in the current partners exchange nametags and choose different partners. Repeat the process twice.

5. At the conclusion of the fourth sharing, ask the participants to introduce themselves as the person whose nametag they are wearing. (Give everyone an opportunity to set the record straight if and when necessary!)

Lesson: This is a reminder of how easily information can become confused when it is passed from one person to another.

I Never Knew That

Objective:

To learn something new about each other *(This activity is a good one to use when students are already acquainted with one another.)*

You Will Need:

- recipe cards or similar cards
- pencils

Directions:

1. Pass out a card and a pencil to each student.

2. Ask each student to write one thing about her/himself that no one else in the room knows. Instruct them not to write their names on the cards. (Be sure to tell them that this piece of information will be revealed.)

3. When all students have finished, collect the cards in a container.

4. Now ask each student to take a card from the container, being sure to replace it if they take his or her own.

5. Ask students to find the person whose card they now have and then ask a few questions to uncover more information.

6. When everyone has finished, ask each student to introduce the person whose card they have, using the information as an opener.

> **Lesson:** The more we learn about each other, the better we understand one another.

Conflict Can Be Positive

Objective:

To teach students that conflict can be positive

You Will Need:

- chart paper and markers, or
- chalkboard and chalk

Directions:

Remind students of the guidelines for brainstorming:

Call out anything that comes to mind.
There are no right or wrong answers.
Do not judge responses.

1. Write the word *conflict* on chart paper. Ask students to brainstorm whatever comes to mind when they hear this word.

2. Once you have about 30 words, stop and ask the students whether, if someone walked into the room, he/she would notice anything unusual about the words. Do they have anything in common? (Someone will probably say that they all seem negative.)

3. Ask students if conflict has to be negative. Ask if they can think of anything that can be positive about conflict.

4. Ask students to share with the group a time when something positive happened to them as a result of a conflict.

5. Close with a discussion about how conflict can provide us with opportunities to learn and grow.

> **Lesson:** Many great ideas and inventions
> have resulted from conflict.

Responses to Conflict

Objectives:

To teach students that there are different ways of reacting or responding to conflict

To teach students that there is not one "correct" response for all situations

You Will Need:

- Conflict Scenarios (see page 75)
- chart paper and markers, or
- chalkboard and chalk

Directions:

1. Ask students to brainstorm ideas in response to the question,

   "How do people usually react to conflict?" Write the responses on chart paper or on the chalkboard, placing them in columns according to whether they are passive, aggressive or collaborative. (Do not put the categories on the chart paper at this time.)

PASSIVE	AGGRESSIVE	COLLABORATIVE*
ignore it	fight	talk it out
walk away	spread rumours	mediate
run	hurt them	think about their side
give in	spit	talk to a teacher

Depending on the level of the students, you may wish to use "problem solving" here.

2. When the students have contributed all of their ideas, write the headings above the columns and discuss the three ways in which people usually react in conflict situations.

3. Ask students which way of reacting they think is best. (Given the setting, most will say that collaboration is best.) Then offer the following scenario and discuss it briefly.

continued...

You are walking down an unfamiliar street at night. You are alone. Suddenly, you see the shadows of four large people walking across the street. They start to come over saying that they want your hat.

4. Review with the students that there is not one right way to resolve all conflicts. Tell students that you want them to try each of the three styles: Passive, Aggressive and Collaborative. Divide them into small groups and give each group a copy of the Conflict Scenarios. Ask each group to choose one of the scenarios and make up skits using each of the three styles to resolve the conflict. Let them know that they will be asked to perform one of their skits for the class.

5. Have students come back to the large group and ask each group to perform one of the skits using a particular style of response. Ask them for their comments about the exercise and again review that there are different styles of conflict resolution, that it is best to choose the style that best suits each conflict, and that it is entirely appropriate in certain circumstances to have a passive response – that is: walk away.

Scenario A:

A friend of yours often borrows your French dictionary and forgets to return it. Last night when you were about to do your French homework, your book was not in your bag. You think your friend took it and forgot to put it back.

Scenario B:

A student on your basketball team is making rude comments about a friend of yours. It is beginning to bother you and you want to do something to make him stop.

Scenario C:

One of your friends is always late. This morning you planned to meet her on the way to school and you had to wait an extra 15 minutes before she showed up. This made you angry.

> **Lesson:** There are different ways of reacting to conflict. Although the problem-solving way is usually best, sometimes it is good to walk away.

Do We Ever Learn?

Objectives:

To identify the reasons why people fight or argue

To identify some of the common methods used to handle conflict

You Will Need:

- chart paper and markers, or
- chalkboard and chalk

Directions:

1. Explain to the students that you would like them to think about some of the things people argue about and how these situations are typically handled.

2. Create three groups. Give each group chart paper and a marker.

3. Ask the first group to list things that children usually argue about and how they handle these arguments.

4. Do the same for the other groups, using adults for group two and world leaders for group three.

5. Allow enough time for each of the groups to come up with a comprehensive list.

6. Reassemble as a large group. Ask each group to share their ideas and hang the charts on the wall.

For discussion:

"Are there any things children, adults and world leaders all argue about?"

"Are there any common ways in which all three groups handle their arguments?" (There should be some recurring conflicts and ways of handling them in all three charts.)

"What have we learned about handling conflict from childhood, through adulthood and even as world leaders?" (The response to this question is often a resounding "NOTHING!")

> **Lesson:** Mediation offers a creative, peaceful
> means of resolving conflict.

Do You See What I See?

Objective:

To understand that people may view the same event from different perspectives

You Will Need:

- overhead transparency (or enlargement) of "Duck or Rabbit?" and/or "Young Woman or Old Woman?" or an optical illusion of your choice (see pages 76-77)

- overhead projector

Directions:

1. Show the "Duck or Rabbit?" picture to the students using either a transparency or an enlargement.

2. Ask students what they see in the picture.

3. Select one student who sees the Duck and one who sees the Rabbit and ask her/him to point out the features that she/he sees.

4. Do the same for the "Young Woman or Old Woman?" picture.

5. Use the following questions as a guide for discussion:

   "Is there a correct way to see the picture?"

   "How did you feel towards those who saw the picture the same way as you did?"

   "Did you feel differently towards those who saw the other picture?"

   "Why is it important to recognize that there is usually more than one way to look at situations?"

   "How can two people resolve a conflict if they each see the situation from a different point of view?"

Lesson: There are two sides to every story.

The Wolf's Story

Objectives:

To understand the importance of hearing both sides of an issue

To encourage students to think about other familiar stories that are told from one character's perspective

You Will Need:

- "The Wolf's Story" (next page)
- chart paper and markers, or
- chalkboard and chalk

   (optional: props or costume materials)

Directions:

1. Prior to beginning this activity, draw a simple outline of Little Red Riding Hood on one sheet of chart paper and The Wolf on another.

2. Hang the drawings on the wall/chart stand/chalkboard.

3. Ask students if they have ever heard the story of Little Red Riding Hood.

4. Ask for words to describe Little Red Riding Hood and record these on the drawing

5. Do the same for the wolf.

6. Read "The Wolf's Story." (For added effect, you might make some wolf ears or a mask to wear as you read the story.)

7. Ask the students how they feel about the wolf now. Do the same for Little Red Riding Hood.

8. Ask the students to think about other familiar stories in which one of the characters may have been unfairly portrayed.

> **Lesson:** As mediators, it is important
> to listen to both sides of a story with an open mind.

WOLF'S STORY*

The forest was my home. I lived there, and I cared about it.
I tried to keep it neat and clean.

Then one sunny day, while I was cleaning up some garbage a
camper had left behind, I heard footsteps. I leaped behind a tree
and saw a little girl coming down the trail carrying a basket. I
was immediately suspicious of this little girl because she was
dressed funny – all in red, with her head covered up as if she
didn't want people to know who she was. Naturally, I stopped
to check her out. I asked who she was, where she was going and
where she had come from. She gave me a song and dance
about going to her grandmother's house with a basket of lunch.
She appeared to be a basically honest person, but she was in my
forest, and she certainly looked suspicious with that strange red
getup of hers. So I decided to teach her just how serious it is to
prance through the forest unannounced and dressed funny.

I let her go on her way, but I ran ahead to her grandmother's
house. When I saw that nice old woman, I explained my
problem and she agreed that her granddaughter needed to
learn a lesson all right. The old woman agreed to stay out of
sight until I called her. As some of you already may know, she
hid under the bed.

When the girl arrived, I invited her into the bedroom where I was
in the bed, dressed like the grandmother. The girl came in all
rosy cheeked and said something nasty about my big ears. Now,
I've been insulted before so I made the best of it by suggesting
that my big ears would help me to hear better. What I meant
was that I wanted to pay close attention to what she was saying.
But she made another insulting crack about my bulging eyes.
Now you can see how I was beginning to feel about this girl
who put on such a nice front, but was apparently a nasty person.
Still, I've made it a policy to turn the other cheek, so I told her
that my big eyes helped me to see her better.

continued...

---

*This story is adapted from one that has been used in many books, author unknown.

Her next insult really got to me. I've got a problem with having big teeth, and that little girl made an insulting crack about them. I know that I should have had better control, but I leaped up from that bed and growled that my teeth would help me to eat her better.

Now let's face it, no wolf could ever eat a little girl – everyone knows that. But that crazy girl started running around the house screaming – me chasing her to calm her down. I'd taken off the grandmother clothes, but that only seemed to make it worse. All of a sudden the door came crashing open, and a big lumberjack was standing there with his axe. I looked at him and all of a sudden it became clear that I was in BIG trouble. There was an open window behind me and out I went.

I'd like to say that was the end of it. But that Grandmother never did tell my side of the story. Before long word got around that I was a mean, nasty guy. Everybody started avoiding me. I don't know about that little girl with the funny red outfit, but I didn't live happily ever after.

Effective Listening

Objective:

To have students differentiate between effective and poor listening

You Will Need:

- chart paper and markers, or
- chalkboard and chalk
- copies of page 61 "Active Listening" from the *Peer Mediation Handbook.*

Directions:

1. Explain to the students that we hear a great deal about listening and how important it is. Ask, "What is the difference between hearing and listening? How do we know when someone is listening to us?"

2. Explain that in this activity you will demonstrate the difference between effective and poor listening.

3. In the first role-play, tell a brief story to one of the other adults who is participating in the training session. As you tell your story, the listener exhibits poor listening skills by fidgeting, looking away, interrupting inappropriately, and so on.

4. When the role-play is finished, ask the students to describe what the listener did. (List these on a chart.)

5. Repeat the storytelling role-play. This time the listener exhibits good listening skills by making eye contact, nodding and using other gestures indicating understanding, asking appropriate questions, etc.

6. Again, ask students to describe what the listener did. (Record responses.)

continued...

7. On the first chart write the following title: A GOOD LISTENER DOES NOT… and on the second chart write A GOOD LISTENER…

8. Hand out the "Active Listening" sheets to students. Tell them it is from the *Peer Mediation Handbook* they will be receiving. Review and discuss.

> **Lesson:** It is important for mediators to be good listeners. People like to feel that they are listened to when they speak. This is a sign of respect and trust.

Joe's New Bike

Objectives:

To improve listening and speaking skills

To show how messages can change from one person to another

You Will Need:

■ "Joe's New Bike" (next page)

Directions:

1. Ask for three volunteers who think they are good listeners.

2. Ask two of the volunteers to leave the room. Read "Joe's New Bike" to the whole group, including volunteer #1.

3. Ask volunteer #2 to return and ask volunteer #1 to retell the story from memory.

4. Ask volunteer #3 to return and ask volunteer #2 to retell the story from memory.

5. Ask volunteer #3 to retell the story to the group.

6. Use the following questions for discussion:

   "What happened to the information as it was passed along?"

   "Was anything important left out?"

   "How did that affect the story?"

   "What are rumours?"

   "What happens when a rumour is passed from one person to another?"

continued...

> **Lesson:** A story is best told by the person directly involved – not by a witness.

JOE'S NEW BIKE

Joe finally had enough money to buy the red Cannondale Mountain Bike he had been admiring in the window of the Trail Shop for the past six weeks. It was a lot of money – $225.00 – but Joe had been saving his paper-route earnings for two years.

Joe beamed with pride as he raced home with his new ten-speed bike, down Pine Avenue and past Springvale School, where a group of his friends were playing soccer in Beasley field.

Andrew, his best friend, hurried over to admire the new bike. He asked Joe if he could try the bike and Joe, reluctantly, said he could take it around the block.

When Andrew did not return after 10 minutes, Joe began to worry. He ran to the corner where he could see Andrew, in the distance, trying to straighten out the front rim. Three other boys were gathered around. Joe raced to where Andrew was bent over the bike and started yelling at his friend, only to look up and see his beautiful new bike safely resting against a fence. Andrew grinned as he explained that he had stopped to help Craig who had fallen and damaged his bike.

The One-Minute Report

Objective:

To have students practice active listening skills

You Will Need:

■ "Active Listening" checklist on chart paper or written on the board (see next page)

Directions:

1. Create groups of three: listener, speaker and observer.

2. Explain that each student will have an opportunity to talk for one minute on any topic. Each student will take a turn being the speaker, listener and observer. The listener is to listen attentively without interrupting, but giving non-verbal encouragement. After the speaker has finished, the listener will summarize the story as accurately as possible. The observer will observe the listener and make comments about their observations.

3. Continue until all students have had a turn at being speaker, listener, and observer.

continued...

> **Lesson:** Being able to summarize correctly what someone says is an important skill for a mediator. When students in conflict come to you as a peer mediator, they must feel that you are really listening. This means that you care about what the person is saying and feeling. This type of listening is called *active listening*. It means listening without interrupting or judging.

Active Listening Checklist

A mediator demonstrates active listening by:

- facing the speaker
- making eye contact
- listening without interrupting
- using non-verbal encouragement
  (head nodding, facial gestures)
- asking questions to clarify
- summarizing what was said

Open Questions

Objective:

To help students learn to ask questions that are non-judgmental

You Will Need:

- one copy of "Open Questions" worksheet for each student (see page 78)

- pencils

Directions:

1. Explain to the students that they will practice asking questions that will help the disputants tell the complete story.

2. Take a pencil from one of the students and say, "Did you steal this pencil?" (The student will say "No.")

3. Explain that this is a closed question and that closed questions allow for a yes or no answer and in many cases they place blame.

4. Ask students to suggest a better question about the pencil. (example: "Can you tell me where you got that pencil?")

5. Explain that this is an open question. Open questions allow the person to respond in a way that helps to get all of her/his thoughts or feelings out. Open questions do not place blame.

6. Read the following closed questions aloud to the group and ask for volunteers to rephrase them as open questions.

   "Did you break his radio?" "Did you call him a liar?"

   Possible rephrases:
   "What happened to the radio?"
   "What did you say about him when you spoke to your friends?"

continued...

7. Pass out the Open Questions worksheet. Review the list of 'good openers' on the bottom of the sheet, then have students, alone or in small groups, turn the closed questions into open questions

8. When most students are finished, ask for volunteers to share their responses.

Lesson: As mediators, it is important to be non-judgemental.

Listening for Feelings

Objectives:

To learn to identify the feelings of a speaker

To increase the students' vocabulary of emotions

You Will Need:

- list of "Listening for Feelings" statements (see pages 79-80)
- chart paper and markers, or
- chalkboard and chalk

Directions:

1. Tell the students that it is important to listen to people's words but it is also important to listen for feelings.

2. Cut Listening for Feelings into sentence strips and distribute randomly.

3. Ask students to read each statement aloud to the group, and ask the others to identify the feeling that is behind the words.

4. Ask students offer words to describe the feelings, record them on chart paper.

5. Encourage students to use a broader range of vocabulary to describe feelings.

> **Lesson:** Sometimes you may need to help a disputant when he/she is trying to find the right word to describe his/her feelings.

Nonverbal Communication

Objective:

To demonstrate that we often communicate our feelings with body language

You Will Need:

Cards labelled with the following words: (You may wish to add a few of your own.)

Angry   Frustrated   Proud   Sad   Hurt   Worried   Excited   Bored

Directions:

1. Enter the room in an angry manner – slam the door, stomp your feet, cross your arms, frown – then say, "I am so happy that you are all here today. We are going to do a fun activity."

2. Ask the students how they felt about your words. Did they believe you? Were they comfortable? How else were you communicating?

3. Discuss the concept of body language. Explain that sometimes the words we speak are not consistent with our body language.

4. Ask for volunteers to demonstrate through body language the feelings written on the cards. Have students identify the feelings demonstrated.

5. Discuss the importance of using positive body language as mediators. For example, if a mediator rolled her eyes during a session, that would convey a negative message.

Lesson: As mediators, you will need to be attuned to the body language of the disputants. This will help you understand how they are feeling.

"I" Messages

Objective:

To teach students a way of expressing their thoughts and feelings in a non-aggressive manner

You Will Need:

- chart paper and markers, or
- chalkboard and chalk
- role-play scripts (see page 81)
- two volunteers who have rehearsed the role-plays in advance
- Compose an "I" Message worksheet (see page 82)

Directions:

1. Begin with an example of the difference between an "I" Message and a "You" Message. Ask the volunteers to act out the following skit:

   Skit 1: "You" Message

   LAURA: I can't believe you forgot to bring in the poster. You are so forgetful! You are always late and never have anything done on time. Now how are we going to do our presentation?

   PETRA: Well, you wouldn't help me until last night. I was up late because of you and so I slept in this morning. I was in such a rush that I forgot the poster. It's not my fault.

2. After this role-play ask students what they observed both in terms of language and body language.

3. Explain that this is a "You" Message. A "You" Message usually expresses anger or blame and criticizes the other person. People often react to a "You" message by defending themselves and finding a way to counterattack.

4. Ask the children if they think Laura and Petra will be able to resolve this conflict. After a discussion, ask the volunteers to act out the second skit.

continued...

Skit 2: "I" Message

LAURA: Petra, I am very upset because we don't have the poster. We can't do our presentation without it. I wish there was a way we could get it before this afternoon.

PETRA: I'm sorry that I forgot it. I was in such a rush this morning. I know that we need it to do our presentation. Maybe my mom can bring it over on her way to work.

5. Discuss the difference between these two skits. Explain that an "I" Message tells how you feel without blaming or attacking the other person. When we use "I" Messages, the other person realizes that we are upset, and because we are not blaming them they are more likely to try to come up with a win–win solution.

6. On chart paper, print the following "I" message formula. Hand out the "I" Message Worksheet and brainstorm "I" message answers to the first situation. If time permits, have students work on other situations, or they may take them away to practice on.

_____, I feel _____

when you _____

_____

because _____

_____

and I want/wish/would like _____

_____

_____

Lesson: During the mediation process there may be situations where it is necessary to give one of the disputants an "I" Message.

Introducing Mediation

Objective:

To introduce students to the mediation process

You Will Need:

- chart paper and markers, or
- chalkboard and chalk
- two experienced mediators
- three adult volunteers

Directions:

1. Before this activity, arrange with two of the adult volunteers to have an argument that will seem realistic to the students. Prompt the adults to start arguing at the back of the room while you are making some comments. During the argument role-play, the third adult should jump in and take sides, give advice, not listen carefully, impose solutions, yell, and so on.

2. At some point, stop the argument and pose the following questions for discussion. Make a list of the responses on the board or chart. Later, title this list *A Mediator Does Not...*

   "What things did you see the helper doing?"

   "How did the disputants respond?"

   "How did disputants seem to feel as a result of the help they received?"

   "What might the helper have done differently?"

   "Was the problem solved?"

3. Next ask the experienced mediators to demonstrate a mediation with the two disputants.

4. At the conclusion of the mediation, ask the same discussion questions. This time title the list: *A Mediator...*

continued...

> **Lesson:** As a peer mediator you will listen to the disputants and help them come up with solutions to their conflict. You will be open-minded, fair, calm and respectful.

The Mediation Process

Objective:

To introduce the mediation process by explaining the steps through a role-play demonstration

You Will Need:

- four copies of "The Puzzling Case" (see page 86-89)

- an outline of the three stages in the mediation process (see next pages). The three stages may be presented on chart paper (prepared in advance) or projected (see pages 83-85)

- four student volunteers who have been assigned parts in "The Puzzling Case."

Directions:

1. Prior to this activity, select four students who are willing to dramatize the role-play "The Puzzling Case." Allow these volunteers time to rehearse prior to the demonstration.

2. Ask the volunteers to role-play "The Puzzling Case" in front of the group. Freeze the action after:

   - Introduction and Ground Rules

   - Telling the Story

   - Finding Solutions

3. At each of these pauses, refer to the steps on the chart paper and clarify any questions.

Point out to the students that the peer mediators take turns when working through the process.

continued...

> **Lesson:** The mediation process is quite simple.
> With experience, you will find that it becomes easy and natural.

STAGE ONE • Introduction and Ground Rules

Introduce yourselves and explain your role as mediators.

We are here to help you talk about your problem but we will not judge who is right or wrong. We will help you solve your problem but we will not tell you what to do.

Explain that you will keep everything said during the mediation confidential.

When the mediation is over, we will not talk about what was said during the mediation session with anyone else. Will you also agree to keep this session confidential? It is OK to tell your friends that you have resolved this problem.

Have the disputants agree to the following ground-rules:

Do you agree to listen without interrupting?

Do you agree to speak respectfully without name-calling or putdowns?

Do you agree to tell the truth?

Do you agree to try hard to solve the problem?

STAGE TWO • Telling the Story

Ask disputant #1 to tell what happened.

Summarize what was said.

Ask disputant #1 how s/he feels about what happened.

Summarize the feelings.

Ask disputant #2 to tell what happened.

Summarize what was said.

Ask disputant #2 how s/he feels about what happened.

Ask each disputant if there is anything else he/she would like to say about what happened.

Summarize the problem

continued...

STAGE THREE • Finding Solutions

Ask disputant #1, "What can you do to solve this problem?"

Ask disputant #2, "What can you do to solve this problem?"

Summarize the solutions that have been suggested.

Get agreement to a solution from both disputants.

Ask disputant #1, "What would you do differently if a problem like this happened again?"

Ask disputant #2, "What would you do differently if a problem like this happened again?"

Congratulate the disputants for solving their problem.

Fill out the report form and ask the disputants to sign it.

Good Resolutions

Objective:

To make students aware of what makes a realistic, effective resolution

You Will Need:

- chart paper and markers, or
- chalkboard and chalk
- "Good Resolutions Checklist" (see next page)

Directions:

1. Explain to the students that, as mediators, they will need to know what makes a good resolution and how to work with students to help them find a resolution that is workable.

2. Give the following example:

   One of the disputants has spilled ink on his friend's winter jacket. He suggests that he will buy a new jacket for his friend.

   Is this a good resolution?
   Why or why not?

3. Ask students to come up with aspects of a good resolution. Record their ideas. When all ideas have been offered, refer them to the "Good Resolutions Checklist." Tell them that this page is also in their *Peer Mediation Handbook*.

4. Discuss the items on the checklist to be sure students understand the rationale for each.

continued...

Good Resolution Checklist

☐ Is the resolution realistic? Does it tell:

   ☐ When?

   ☐ Where?

   ☐ How?

   ☐ Who?

☐ Do both disputants take responsibility for making it work?

☐ Can both disputants do what they promise?

☐ Will the resolution solve the problem?

Chapter 3

Reviewing, Practicing, and Getting Started

A s the students' training is nearly finished it is time to bring the training process to a close, give them a chance to role-play some situations, and review their new responsibilities as peer mediators.

Peer Mediation Handbook

You Will Need:

A copy of the *Peer Mediation Handbook* for each student (see pages 57-67)

Copies of the forms they will be expected to use (see pages 72, 73)

Directions:

Tell the students that training has been completed and that it is time for them to "graduate." Hand out the *Peer Mediation Handbook*, and go over each page as a review of the training they have just received. Sign and have them sign The Mediator's Promise (page 58).

Introduce the forms they will be dealing with to report on mediation, and such details as when/where mediation will take place, and so on.

Tell the students that they will next have an opportunity to practice mediating and observing, as well as assuming the roles of disputants.

Mediation Role-Play

You Will Need:

Copies of role-plays (see pages 90-92)

Directions:

The role-plays provided describe conflicts that I have witnessed. However, in your school there may be problems of a different nature. If it is more appropriate, simply use the situations provided as models to create your own.

With prepared role-plays on hand, proceed as follows:

1. Divide the students into groups of four.

2. In each group, ask two students to play the role of mediators and the other two, the disputants.

3. Give each of the disputants a copy of one of the character's stories.

4. Ask the students who will be playing the mediator roles to use the script in their handbooks.

5. Have the groups find a quiet place and, after the disputants have read their stories, stage mediation to resolve the problem.

6. When the groups have finished, invite them back to the large group and ask if any of the groups would like to demonstrate their mediation.

   (This will provide an opportunity to review the steps, clarify misunderstandings, answer questions, etc.)

Students' Questions and Concerns

Refer each student to the section in their handbook titled "Commonly Asked Questions." Discuss "What do I do if" with the students informally, and answer any other questions they may have. Review 'More Questions and Answers,' below and in the student handbook, pages 65-66, and have students fill in the blanks provided with the answers your school's policies dictate.

More Questions and Answers

Will I have to step in when I witness an argument or a fight?

NO, you will not be expected to step in when you witness a conflict.

(It is recommended that all referrals to mediation be made through an adult. It is unfair to expect students to determine what should be referred to mediation and what is best handled by an adult. In cases involving physical violence, most school administrators deal with these incidents or disputes according to the protocols in the school discipline policy.)

How much time will the mediation sessions take?

This is a difficult question to answer because of the many variables involved. On average, a mediation session at the elementary level takes about 20 to 25 minutes. If it seems to be taking longer, you may need to talk to your coordinator. Since most disputes are relatively simple and the disputants are there because they have agreed to participate, the process should be quite efficient.

Where will the mediations take place?

Ideally, the peer mediation program should have a room of its own. If at all possible, this room would be near the principal's office or the classroom or room of the program coordinator. Within the mediation room you will need a table and four chairs.

(It is comforting for the mediators to know that adult assistance is close at hand should it be required.)

What do we do with the reports?

The reports are intended for record keeping and tracking purposes. Keep the completed reports in a file or binder in the mediation room or in another place that will ensure that they are not easily accessible to anyone else. The reports can be destroyed periodically.

(The reports should not be placed into the students' cumulative records.)

Will I miss a lot of class time?

Very often, conflicts occur at recess and lunchtime. The mediators on duty usually handle these conflicts as they occur.

Your teachers will make a decision about whether or not mediation can take place during class time. If they decide that mediations can take place during class time, yes, you may miss some time.

Remember, one of the reasons that you were chosen to be a mediator is because you are a responsible student. This means that you will take responsibility for making up any missed class work.

Parents' and Teachers' Questions and Concerns

With the students trained and ready to start mediating, take some time with other staff or administration to consider the following questions and concerns that are sometimes raised by teachers or parents.

Will student mediators miss a lot of class time?

Deciding whether or not to hold mediation sessions during class time is a school-based decision to be made collaboratively with staff.

Students in dispute may find it difficult to concentrate on the lesson or task at hand as they expend their emotional energy thinking of ways to get even or simply focusing on their feelings of anger, frustration, etc. Once again, the referral is made through the teacher who needs to make a judgment call based on the particular incident in question. Keep in mind that one of the criteria for the selection of students to be trained in mediation is that they be willing to take responsibility for catching up on missed class work.

Will students request mediation in order to avoid "punishment?"

Most interpersonal conflicts between students do not involve a violation of a school rule. The purpose of mediation is to resolve disputes.

When a student is discovered writing graffiti on the walls of the washroom or throwing a rock at a classmate, obviously mediation is not appropriate and these incidents are dealt with according to school policy. Mediation does not compromise the school's discipline policy. It is important that work be done with all students in the school to enhance their understanding of mediation and its applications.

What about disputes involving violence?

Schools deal with these incidents according to the policies developed internally. Often, students involved in these incidents, if serious in nature, are suspended from school for a period of one to five days. However, when these students return, they usually do so with the dispute left unresolved and it may flare up again. It would certainly be beneficial to offer mediation to allow the students an opportunity to work out the unresolved dispute between them.

Does the coordinator need to be present during the mediation sessions?

One of the advantages of running a mediation program is that the disputants feel freer talking to their peers than a teacher or administrator. Knowing that the role of the mediators is one of facilitation, not judgment or punishment, students in dispute will feel more comfortable in telling their stories openly and honestly.

Once the mediators are trained and comfortable with their role and the process, there is really no need for an adult to be in the room during the mediation session. Initially, after training, the coordinator may wish to observe the mediators in action in order to give feedback and suggestions. As a courtesy, it is good practice to ask the disputants if they would allow you (the coordinator) to observe.

During the session, it is very important not to intervene, as difficult as that may be at times!

How do we respond to the parents of the mediators when they express concern about the safety of their children during and after the mediation sessions?

First, as mentioned previously, an adult should always be close at hand when a session is underway. Potentially "dangerous" conflicts are not sent to mediation.

Because peer mediators do not take sides, or impose punishments, experience has shown that the disputants are usually grateful to have an opportunity to talk through their problem and it would be most unusual for any form of retaliation to take place after the mediation session.

*The mediators' promise of confidentiality is important in
mediation. The disputants come to appreciate the process
and develop a genuine respect for the mediators.*

*Once parents have developed an understanding of the mediation
program, they are often its most vocal supporters!*

Appendices

Appendices

Contents

To enlarge the following pages to 8.5" X 11" set the photocopier at 121%

NOTE

To assemble Peer Mediation Handbooks

- Copy pages 57-67 inclusive on one side of the paper only.

- To mask book page and title footer, cover before copying.

- Consider using colored paper for covers.

- Staple pages together on left edge, or use commercial binder covers.

- Consider making a few extra for possible losses.

PEER MEDIATION HANDBOOK

This book belongs to

_____

_____

_____

Congratulations on being chosen to become a peer mediator. Your teachers and peers have selected you because you have the qualities that are necessary for being an effective mediator.

MEDIATOR'S PROMISE

I Promise

- To be fair and honest
- To keep what is said in mediation sessions confidential
- To resolve my own conflicts peacefully
- To make up work I miss in class
- To attend mediator meetings
- To serve as a mediator for at least one year

Student's Signature: _____

Parent's Signature: _____

Teacher's Signature: _____

Date:_____

What Is Mediation?

Mediation is a voluntary process that helps people in conflict resolve their problem.

Mediation offers a "win - win" means of resolving conflicts cooperatively. Mediators help people who are having a conflict listen to each other and find a solution to their problem. The goal of mediation is to help each person listen to the other person's side of the story so that she/he can see the whole story and not only her/his point of view. The disputants (people having the conflict) are responsible for finding a fair solution to their problem.

As a peer mediator you will help students in your school resolve their problems. You will work with another peer mediator as a team. You will use good problem-solving and communication skills to help others solve their problems.

Mediation is

■ A process to help solve conflicts between two or more people.

■ A process by which the disputants decide on their own solutions to the conflict.

■ A process in which the disputants feel the solutions are fair.

■ A voluntary process.

■ A process in which everyone is shown respect.

■ A process that works on the concept of fairness rather than power.

■ A process that respects the confidentiality of the people involved.

Peer Mediator Guidelines

A mediator ...

- Listens carefully ... does not interrupt.
- Communicates clearly.
- Asks questions for understanding.
- Treats each person with respect.
- Remains neutral ... does not take sides.
- Does not give advice or offer an opinion.
- Does not look for innocence or guilt.
- Helps the disputants find a solution to their problem.

Active Listening

Active listening is when a listener tries to understand both the facts and feelings of the speaker. The listener then restates what s/he has heard to make sure s/he has heard correctly.

A good listener ...

- listens without interrupting
- uses non-verbal facial expressions
- makes eye contact
- asks questions to clarify

A good listener does not ...

- interrupt
- offer advice
- give her/his opinion
- bring up similar feelings or problems
- agree or disagree with what is being said

Some suggestions when trying to clarify:

Tell me more about…
Please explain…
So what you are saying is…
In other words…
What I understand you to be saying is…
What do you feel is not being understood…
Correct me if I'm wrong…

Active Listening Observer Checklist

Although in most day-to-day conversations, we do not summarize what we hear, mediators do summarize the stories they hear from the disputants. This is done so that everyone is very clear about what happened. If something is not clear, the disputant has an opportunity to clarify by adding additional information or correcting something that may have been misunderstood.

Listener:

- Looked attentively at the speaker
- Listened without interrupting
- Used non-verbal encouragement
  (head nodding, facial gestures, etc.)
- Used verbal responses (uh-huh, yes, etc.)
- Summarized accurately what was said

The Mediation Process

Introductions and Ground Rules

- Introduce yourselves and explain your role as mediators.
- Have the disputants agree to four ground rules:
  1. listen without interrupting
  2. speak respectfully – no name-calling or put downs
  3. agree to tell the truth
  4. agree to try hard to solve the problem
- Explain that you will keep everything said during the mediation confidential.

Telling the Story

- Ask disputant #1 to tell what happened.
- Summarize what was said.
- Ask disputant #1 how he or she feels about what happened.
- Summarize the feelings.
- Ask disputant #2 to tell what happened.
- Summarize what was said.
- Ask disputant #2 how he or she feels about what happened.
- Summarize the feelings.
- Ask if either disputant has anything more to add.
- Summarize the problem.

Finding Solutions

- Ask disputant #1 what he or she can do to solve the problem.
- Ask disputant #2 what he or she can do to solve the problem.
  - Summarize the solutions.
  - Get agreement to a solution from both disputants.
  - Ask disputant #1 what he or she would do differently if this problem happened again.
- Ask disputant #2 what he or she would do differently if this problem happened again.
  - Congratulate the disputants for solving their problem.
  - Fill out the report form.

Checklist for a Good Resolution

☐ Is the resolution specific enough? Does it tell:

    ☐ When?
    ☐ Where?
    ☐ How?
    ☐ Who?

☐ Is the resolution balanced? Do both disputants share responsibility for making it work?

☐ Can both disputants do what they promise?

☐ Will the resolution solve the problem?

Commonly Asked Questions

What do I do if

One of the disputants will not cooperate?

> *Ask if he or she really wants to be there. Remind him/her of the ground rules and emphasize that the process will only work if the ground rules are followed. If the disputant continues to be uncooperative, you will have to end the mediation and tell your coordinator (teacher in charge of the mediation program) or the teacher who made the referral.*

My best friend wants me to mediate a dispute?

> *Explain to your friend that a mediator does not take sides so it would be better to ask someone else to mediate.*

One of the disputants becomes aggressive?

> *Stop the mediation and get a teacher.*

One of the disputants wants to talk about other conflicts that happened in the past?

> *Explain that the mediation is to resolve the problem that just occurred, not problems from the past.*

Someone asks me to tell what happened during a mediation session?

> *Explain that everything said during the mediation session is confidential and therefore you cannot discuss it. (You may need to explain what confidential means.)*

The disputants cannot resolve the conflict?

> *Mediation is not always successful. Simply thank the disputants for trying to resolve their conflict through mediation and tell them that you will have to report the outcome to your coordinator.*

More Questions and Answers

Will I have to step in when I witness an argument or a fight?

> *NO, you will not be expected to step in when you witness a conflict.*

_____

_____

How much time will the mediation sessions take?

On average, a mediation session at the elementary level takes about 20 to 25 minutes.

_____

_____

_____

_____

Where will the mediations take place?

_____

_____

_____

_____

What do we do with the reports?

_____

_____

_____

_____

Will I miss a lot of class time?

Very often, conflicts occur at recess and lunchtime. The mediators on duty usually handle these conflicts as they occur.

Your teachers will make a decision about whether or not mediation can take place during class time. If they decide that mediations can take place during class time, yes, you may miss some time.

Remember, one of the reasons that you were chosen to be a mediator is because you are a responsible student. This means that you will take responsibility for making up any missed class work.

Glossary

Confidential   private or secret

Conflict   an argument or disagreement between two or more people

Disputant   a person involved in a conflict

Mediation   a voluntary process for resolving conflict in which a neutral third party helps the disputants reach an agreeable win/win solution

Neutral   not siding with one person or another

Peer Mediator   a student who serves as a mediator in his or her school

Summarize   restate the main points

School Letterhead

Date_____

Dear _____:

Your child has been selected to become a participant in a peer mediation program that will be initiated in school this fall.

A training camp has been organized for the weekend of_____
_____ at _____ located in _____.

There will be ten representatives from each of the schools listed above attending this camp. The students will be accompanied by teacher coordinators who will work with the students within their own schools as the program grows throughout the year.

Peer mediation is being introduced in our schools as an alternate way to address the problem of settling disputes and reducing conflict. The mediation process is simple. Students trained as mediators meet with the students in conflict to help them work out their differences in a positive and constructive manner. The mediators work in pairs with the disputants in a private setting within the school. This program has met with success in a number of Canadian schools. The success of the program is due in part to the non-judgmental approach and the absence of an adult authority figure.

The students chosen to participate have qualities and skills that will ensure the success of the program. We ask for your permission to include your child in the peer mediation program.

Further details will be available in the near future. If you have any questions please call the school, and I will be happy to address any concerns or provide any additional information you wish.

_____
School Coordinator

- -

I _____ give permission for my child

_____to participate in a weekend peer mediation

training camp at _____, on _____.

Date:_____ Parent's Signature:_____

Peer Mediation Application Form

Name _____

Grade _____

Teacher _____

Date _____

Have you ever been in a leadership position?
(Cubs, Guides, Youth groups, etc.) _____

_____

_____

_____

Why do you want to become a peer mediator? _____

_____

_____

_____

Why do you think you would be a good peer mediator? _____

_____

_____

_____

Signature: _____

Parent's Signature: _____

This is a sample training agenda for a weekend retreat.
(Beginning on Friday evening and ending on Sunday at noon.)

Mediation Training Agenda

Friday

6:00 - 7:30	Arrival, cabin assignments
7:30 - 8:30	Welcome (general introduction, logistics)
	Goals for training session (brief agenda review)
	Web Game
	Getting to Know You Bingo
	(Job sign-up)
8:30 - 9:15	Storytelling and snack

Saturday

7:15 - 8:00	Wake-up/Morning walk
8:00 - 8:30	Breakfast
9:00 - 9:15	Make nametags
9:15 - 10:00	*Role of the Mediator* (role play demonstration)
10:00 - 10:30	*The Puzzling Case* (to review steps)
10:30 - 10:45	Break and snack
10:45 - 11:30	Active Listening
	Joe's New Bike
	Effective Listening
	One Minute Report
11:30 - 12:00	*"I" Messages*
12:00 - 1:30	Lunch and outdoor activity
1:30 - 2:30	The Nature of Conflict
	Do We Ever Learn?
	The Wolf's Story

2:30 - 3:00	Break and snack
3:00 - 3:30	Role-play practice in groups of four (using prepared scenarios)
3:30 - 4:00	Demonstration and debrief
4:00 - 4:30	Open Questions
4:30 - 5:00	Good Resolutions
5:00 - 6:00	Free time
5:15 - 6:15	Dinner
6:15 - 9:15	Walk, games, stories, free time
9:15	Snack

Sunday

7:15 – 8:00	Wake-up/Morning walk
8:00 - 8:30	Breakfast
8:30 - 9:00	Empty cabins, assemble belongings for loading into cars
9:00 - 9:15	Review steps in mediation process
9:15 - 9:45	Role-play practice (make up own conflict situation)
9:45 - 10:15	Discussion and questions
10:15 - 10:30	Pledge and certificates
10:30 - 11:00	Pack and depart

Mediator Report Form

Date: _____

Mediators:_____   _____

Students Involved in Conflict:

Student A: _____   Grade: _____

Student B: _____   Grade: _____

Type of Conflict:

☐ Fighting   ☐ Friendship   ☐ Teasing

☐ Name-Calling   ☐ Threatening   ☐ Property

Other _____

Conflict Resolved: ☐ Yes   ☐ No

Student A agrees to: _____

_____

_____

Student B agrees to: _____

_____

_____

Signature Student A_____

Signature Student B_____

AGREEMENT

between

_____

and

_____

We have taken part in a mediation session and we have voluntarily agreed to the following:

1. _____

_____

_____

2. _____

_____

_____

3. _____

_____

_____

We believe that this agreement is fair and we agree to live up to it.

Signed: _____

Signed: _____

Date: _____

Getting to Know You Bingo

Is a good swimmer	Has visited another country	Can play a musical instrument	Likes to read
Plays chess	Is left-handed	Writes poetry	Is afraid of the dark
Has more than 3 brothers or sisters	Likes the same sport as you	Put your name here	Likes to cook
Has a friend from another country	Is a good listener	Can speak another language	Has a grandparent living with them

Conflict Scenarios

Scenario A:

A friend of yours often borrows your French dictionary and forgets to return it. Last night when you were about to do your French homework, your book was not in your bag. You think your friend took it and forgot to put it back.

Scenario B:

A student on your basketball team is making rude comments about a friend of yours. It is beginning to bother you and you want to do something to make him stop.

Scenario C:

One of your friends is always late. This morning you planned to meet her on the way to school and you had to wait an extra 15 minutes before she showed up. This made you angry.

Open Questions

Rewrite the following questions as open questions.

1. Did you take his book? _____

_____

_____

_____

_____

2. Why don't you just apologize? _____

_____

_____

3. Are you lying? _____

_____

_____

4. Did you call her a thief? _____

_____

_____

5. Are you jealous of her? _____

_____

_____

Hint: The following are good "openers" when composing open questions or trying to uncover additional information:

Tell me more about...What do you mean by...Correct me if I'm wrong...Please explain...Then what happened...Let's go back to...How do you feel about...What do you feel is not being understood...How did this start...Let me understand... What would you like to happen? What do you need to make everything OK again?

Listening for Feelings

1. Why don't you just leave me alone.

2. A+ - I don't believe it!

3. How will I ever get this finished?

4. I don't need your help. I can do it myself.

5. I just can't figure it out. I give up.

6. Wow. Just four more days until summer vacation!

7. Will you be calling my parents?

8. You never get mad at him, always me.

9. I'm getting a new puppy.

10. I shouldn't have been so mean to her. It wasn't her fault.

11. Leave me alone. Nobody cares what happens to me anyway.

12. Am I doing this right? I don't think I will ever get it finished.

Role-Play Scripts

Skit 1: "You" Message

LAURA: I can't believe you forgot to bring in the poster. You are so forgetful! You are always late and never have anything done on time. Now how are we going to do our presentation?

PETRA: Well, you wouldn't help me until last night. I was up late because of you and so I slept in this morning. I was in such a rush that I forgot the poster. It's not my fault.

Skit 2: "I" Message

LAURA: Petra, I am very upset because we don't have the poster. We can't do our presentation without it. I wish there was a way we could get it before this afternoon.

PETRA: I'm sorry that I forgot it. I was in such a rush this morning. I know that we need it to do our presentation. Maybe my mom can bring it over on her way to work.

Compose an "I" Message

With practice, "I" Messages are easy to use. Try writing "I" Messages for the following situations.

The disputants keep interrupting each other. You have reminded them of the ground rules several times. _____

_____

_____

_____

You hear two opposing stories from the disputants. _____

_____

_____

_____

One of the disputants is very angry. She says, "You won't believe me anyway." _____

_____

_____

During the mediation, your co-mediator did most of the talking. You are upset that she did not give you a chance to participate.

_____

_____

Hint: A helpful formula is _____,

I feel_____ when you _____

because _____

and I want/wish/would like _____

_____

_____

© 2002 Portage & Main Press. May be reproduced for classroom use.

Three Stages of the Mediation Process

STAGE ONE

Introduction and Ground Rules

Introduce yourselves and explain your role as mediators.

We are here to help you talk about your problem but we will not judge who is right or wrong. We will help you solve your problem but we will not tell you what to do.

Explain that you will keep everything said during the mediation confidential.

When the mediation is over, we will not talk about what was said during the mediation session with anyone else. Will you also agree to keep this session confidential? It is OK to tell your friends that you have resolved this problem.

Have the disputants agree to the following ground-rules:

Do you agree to listen without interrupting?
Do you agree to speak respectfully without name-calling or putdowns?
Do you agree to tell the truth?
Do you agree to try hard to solve the problem?

STAGE TWO

Telling the Story

Ask disputant #1 to tell what happened.

Summarize what was said.

Ask disputant #1 how s/he feels about what happened.

Summarize the feelings.

Ask disputant #2 to tell what happened.

Summarize what was said.

Ask disputant #2 how s/he feels about what happened.

Ask each disputant if there is anything else he/she would like to say about what happened.

Summarize the problem.

STAGE THREE

Finding Solutions

Ask disputant #1, "What can you do to solve this problem?"

Ask disputant #2, "What can you do to solve this problem?"

Summarize the solutions that have been suggested.

Get agreement to a solution from both disputants.

Ask disputant #1, "What would you do differently if a problem like this happened again?"

Ask disputant #2, "What would you do differently if a problem like this happened again?"

Congratulate the disputants for solving their problem.

Fill out the report form and ask the disputants to sign it.

The Puzzling Case

Situation: Andrew has been working on a puzzle during the lunch hour and is almost finished. The puzzle is spread out on the floor in one corner of the classroom. Bianca has been asked by the teacher to finish a mural and needs the floor space that Andrew is using.

Bianca and Andrew are arguing when the lunch monitor walks into the room.

MONITOR:	Looks like you two have a problem. Would you like help solving it?
BIANCA:	Yes, please! I don't have much time to finish this mural.
ANDREW:	I wish you could help. Bianca won't listen to me.
MONITOR:	Well, Marisa and James are the mediators on duty today. Let me go get them. I think they may be able to help.
MARISA:	Hello, our names are Marisa and James. What are your names?
ANDREW:	I'm Andrew.
BIANCA:	And I'm Bianca.
JAMES:	We are student mediators. Our role as mediators is to help you talk about your problem but we will not judge who is right or wrong. Would you like us to help you try to solve your problem?
ANDREW:	Yes, please.
BIANCA:	Yes, and we don't have much time.
MARISA:	We also want you to know that we will keep everything said during this session confidential. We would also like you to agree that you keep what is said during this session confidential.
JAMES:	But it is OK to tell your friends that you have resolved your problem when this session is over.
BIANCA:	OK with me.

ANDREW: Me too.

MARISA: Before we begin, we need you to agree to four rules:
              We want you to listen without interrupting.
              Please speak respectfully – no name-calling or put-
              downs.
              We also want you to agree to tell the truth.
              And it is important that you try hard to solve the
              problem.
              Can you both agree to these rules?

BIANCA: I can.

ANDREW: Me, too.

F R E E Z E THE ACTION
and review steps of Stage ONE on the chart

JAMES: Bianca, will you please tell us what happened?

BIANCA: Ms. Burchell asked me to finish this mural before the
              bell rings. This is the only corner in the room without
              carpet so I need to work here on the floor. Andrew is
              only putting a puzzle together and he won't move.
              This mural is much more important.

JAMES: So, you're saying that you have a mural to finish
              before the bell rings and Andrew won't move the
              puzzle he is working on to let you use this floor space?

BIANCA: Right!

JAMES: How do you feel about this, Bianca?

BIANCA: Well, I feel very frustrated because I need to finish this
              and I am running out of time.

JAMES: You feel frustrated because you are running out of
              time and you have a project to finish?

BIANCA: Exactly.

MARISA: Andrew, will you please tell us what the problem is?

ANDREW: This is a very hard puzzle and I'm almost finished. I
              just can't pick it up and move it. Bianca expects me to
              destroy an hour's work. Besides, I was here first!

MARISA:	So, you want to finish the puzzle you were working on and you can't move it easily.
ANDREW:	Yes, and this is the only floor space that I can use, too.
MARISA:	How do you feel, Andrew?
ANDREW:	I feel angry because Bianca just came over here and told me to move. This puzzle has taken a long time and no one else has been able to do it.
MARISA:	You feel angry because Bianca wants you to move and you would like to finish this puzzle?
ANDREW:	Right!
MARISA:	Is there anything else you would like to tell us about what happened?
BIANCA:	No.
ANDREW:	Just that I was here first and I don't want to start this puzzle all over.
MARISA:	Well, thank you both for telling us what happened. So, the problem seems to be that Andrew has been working on a puzzle on the floor and now the teacher has asked Bianca to make a mural and she needs the space on the floor where Andrew is making the puzzle. All right, let's try to solve this problem.

F R E E Z E THE ACTION
and review steps of Stage TWO on the chart

JAMES:	Bianca, what do you think you could do to solve this problem?
BIANCA:	Well—I suppose I could help Andrew finish the puzzle so that I can work here. I did that puzzle once last year anyway. It wouldn't be too hard for me.
MARISA:	Andrew, what can you do to help solve this problem?
ANDREW:	Maybe Bianca could help me move the puzzle. I don't think we have time to finish it. We could slide a piece of cardboard under it and move it to the table.

JAMES:	Any other ideas?
BIANCA:	I think moving the puzzle is a good idea. Then I still have time to finish this mural.
ANDREW:	I could help you with the mural. I can at least paint in the background.
MARISA:	Do you both agree that moving the puzzle is a good idea?
BIANCA:	Yeah, thanks for your help.
JAMES:	Bianca, what would you do differently if this problem happened again?
BIANCA:	Well—I shouldn't have told Andrew to move. I know that it is a hard puzzle and he was here first.
MARISA:	Andrew?
ANDREW:	Next time I start a puzzle, I'll work on a piece of cardboard so that I can move it easily.
JAMES:	Is your problem solved?
BIANCA and ANDREW (in unison):	Yes!
JAMES:	Congratulations on a successful mediation. We need to fill in a report form and we will come back later when you are finished the mural for your signatures.

F R E E Z E THE ACTION
and review steps of Stage THREE on the chart

Mediation Role-Play

Give this half to Yuko.

The Missing Calculator

Problem:

Jamil and Yuko sit beside each other in class. Ms. Myers, their teacher, has asked each student to buy a calculator for math class. Jamil has not bought his yet so Yuko loaned hers to Jamil over the lunch period. When Yuko comes back from lunch she asks Jamil for her calculator. Jamil says that he put it back on Yuko's desk.

Yuko

Your calculator is missing and you feel Jamil is responsible. You really didn't want to loan it to Jamil in the first place because he had a month to buy his own. He simply didn't bother. Now, math class is about to begin and you need your calculator.

✄ --

Give this half to Jamil.

The Missing Calculator

Problem:

Jamil and Yuko sit beside each other in class. Ms. Myers, their teacher, has asked each student to buy a calculator for math class. Jamil has not bought his yet so Yuko loaned hers to Jamil over the lunch period. When Yuko comes back from lunch she asks Jamil for her calculator. Jamil says that he put it back on Yuko's desk.

Jamil

You don't know what happened to Yuko's calculator. You put it back on her desk and when you came back from the washroom, Yuko had returned from lunch and asked for her calculator. The calculator costs $6.00, and your mother has not given you the money yet even though you have asked her for it a number of times. You are embarrassed to tell Ms. Myers that you do not have money to buy the calculator.

Give this half to Leah.

The Messy Desk

Problem:

Leah and Danielle share a desk. They are in grade 6 and have been friends for a few years. The storage space under the desktop is not divided so Leah, who is a collector, has papers and books spilling over into Danielle's side. Danielle is very neat and organized and is frustrated by continually having to tidy up this storage space. One day, out of frustration, Danielle empties everything onto the floor and is in the process of throwing out a pile of papers when Leah walks into the room.

Leah

You struggle with homework and projects and feel that you need to save rough notes and worksheets in case you need them to complete an assignment. You are upset because you have just failed a math test and Danielle made 96.

Give this half to Danielle

The Messy Desk

Problem:

Leah and Danielle share a desk. They are in grade 6 and have been friends for a few years. The storage space under the desktop is not divided so Leah, who is a collector, has papers and books spilling over into Danielle's side. Danielle is very neat and organized and is frustrated by continually having to tidy up this storage space. One day, out of frustration, Danielle empties everything onto the floor and is in the process of throwing out a pile of papers when Leah walks into the room.

Danielle

Being neat has been emphasized by your mother for as long as you can remember. Although you like Leah, you cannot understand why she can't keep her side of the desk in order. Her papers that spill over into your side look like they belong in the trash. You are fed up and decide to clean out the entire storage space.

Give this half to Arup.

The Project

Problem:

Arup and Jane have a science project due in two days. Although they are partners, Jane has done most of the work. They are having lunch together and Jane is calling Arup "irresponsible" and "lazy" in front of their friends.

Arup

You did not really like the topic of your project but agreed to it because Jane insisted. Jane seems to be taking the lead; telling you what to do and how to do it. You have your part of the project completed but left it at home because you were late getting up and you forgot it in your rush to get to school.

✂ -

Give this half to Jane.

The Project

Problem:

Arup and Jane have a science project due in two days. Although they are partners, Jane has done most of the work. They are having lunch together and Jane is calling Arup "irresponsible" and "lazy" in front of their friends.

Jane

You have always been interested in whales. Your mother is a biologist and has access to a lot of information. You are very organized and like to have assignments passed in ahead of time. You really wanted to do this project on your own but your teacher assigned everyone to a partner.